# Bicycles now and fifty years ago

Hilary Stone

Bicycles nowadays are different from those made 50 years ago. Compare how they have changed with passenger ships, trains, buses, cars, and aeroplanes.

## Contents

# Why people ride bicycles

## Fifty years ago

### People rode bicycles for lots of reasons.

Lots of people rode bicycles to go to work. They used bicycles to go shopping. Few people drove cars.

⬆ Bicycles were the cheapest way to travel.

Many people also used their bikes for fun at the weekend and for holidays.

# Now

## Most bicycles are ridden for fun nowadays.

Many of our cities are too full of cars so some people use their bikes again for going to work.

⬆ Some families go for rides to keep fit. Many rides are not on the road.

# Different types of bicycle

## Fifty years ago

Roadster bicycles were used by cyclists to go to work and to do the shopping.

⬆ Sports bikes were used by cyclists for racing and for fun.

⬆ Carrier bikes were used to deliver goods.

# Now

The most common type of bicycle nowadays is the mountain bike.

⬆ Mountain bikes are used for racing off-road.

⬆ Some cyclists use folding bikes which can easily be carried around.

⬆ Children often have BMX bicycles or mountain bikes.

# Bicycle racing

## Fifty years ago

Fifty years ago there were three kinds of races.

**Track races** were held on special tracks with special track bicycles with no gears or brakes.

⬆ A British rider, Reg Harris, was several times world champion on the track.

**Time trials** were held on roads. Each rider started the race at a different time. The person who cycled the same distance in the shortest time won.

**Road races** were held on roads.

◀ In road races the riders raced on the road from one place to another.

# Now

## Track racing and time trials are as popular as they were 50 years ago.

There are two kinds of mountain bike racing.

**Downhill racing** is where riders ride very fast down a steep hill.

**Cross-country racing** is where riders all race together around a course.

**Road racing** is very popular. The Tour de France is the most famous road race.

7

# Gears and brakes

Gears can help you go faster and climb hills more easily. Brakes are needed to stop you.

## Fifty years ago

Fifty years ago roadster bicycles often only had three gears. You had to push very hard when there was a steep hill.

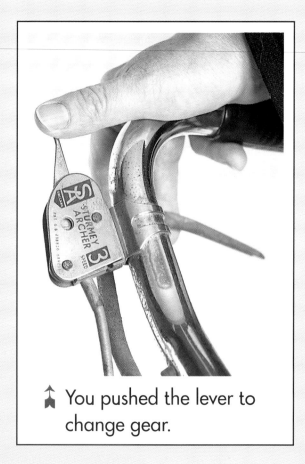

⬆ You pushed the lever to change gear.

⬆ Roadster bikes had rod brakes which were difficult to fix. They did not work very well when it rained.

# Now

Mountain bikes have 21, 24 or even sometimes 27 gears. Some of the gears make it very easy to pedal up the steepest hill.

⬆ Changing gear is easy.

Mountain bikes use special brakes. They can help you stop quickly.

⬆ Road bikes use calliper brakes. The brake blocks work better in the wet.

# Going faster

## Fifty years ago

Fifty years ago the fastest bicycles were those fitted with drop handlebars.

⬆ The drop handlebars helped the rider bend low.

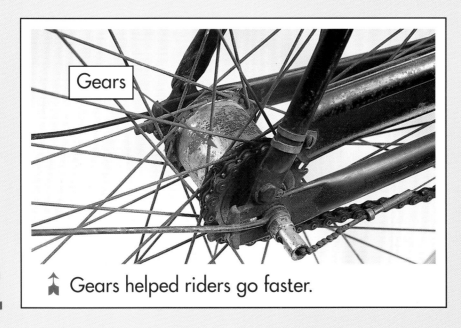

Gears

⬆ Gears helped riders go faster.

# Now

## Nowadays road bicycles still have drop handlebars.

↥ Some bicycles have an extra pair of handlebars so that the rider can bend lower and go through the air quicker.

Bikes which weigh less help the rider go faster.

Racing riders wear special helmets and clothes.

↥ Disc wheels help the rider go very fast.

# Wheels and tyres

Wheels and tyres are one of the most important parts of a bicycle.

## Fifty years ago

Fifty years ago most bicycles wheels had steel rims. They were heavy. Tyres were also quite heavy.

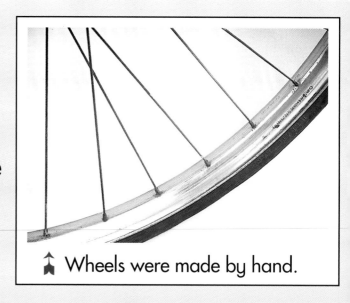

⬆ Wheels were made by hand.

Spokes

Tyre

Hub

Rim

# Now

Most bicycle wheels have aluminium rims. These are lighter than steel. They help riders to go faster. The tyres on road bicycles are lighter and thinner too.

Wheels are often made with a special machine nowadays.

⬆ Mountain bikes use fat, rough tyres. They help the bike go through mud and over rough ground.

# Clothes to cycle in

## Fifty years ago

Fifty years ago road racers used special shirts with pockets in the front to carry their food. They wore special shorts made from wool.

⬆ Some men wore special trousers called plus twos.

# Now

Nowadays most riders wear a helmet to protect their heads if they have an accident.

⬆ Racers wear special shirts with pockets at the back for food. The shirts and the shorts are made from a special stretchy material.

⬆ There are many special clothes now. They are brightly coloured so that car drivers can see the cyclist easily.

# Glossary of words used in this book

**Brakes**           Brakes help the bicycle to stop.

**Disc wheels**      Disc wheels look as if they are made from one piece of material. You cannot see any spokes.

**Gears**            Gears are the parts of a bicycle that can help you go faster or climb steep hills.

**Hub**              The hub is the bit in the middle of a wheel. It allows the wheel to go round.

**Keep fit**         To keep fit is to keep healthy by exercising.

**Off-road**       Off-road is a place that is not on a road where people ride bicycles or drive cars. It can be rough track or a path.

**Rim**              The rim is the edge of the wheel. The tyre is fixed to the rim.